New Course in Practical English

Lesson 12

Finally, here is a simple and enjoyable programme for improving your spelling.... to help you to write with confidence, ease, and speed!

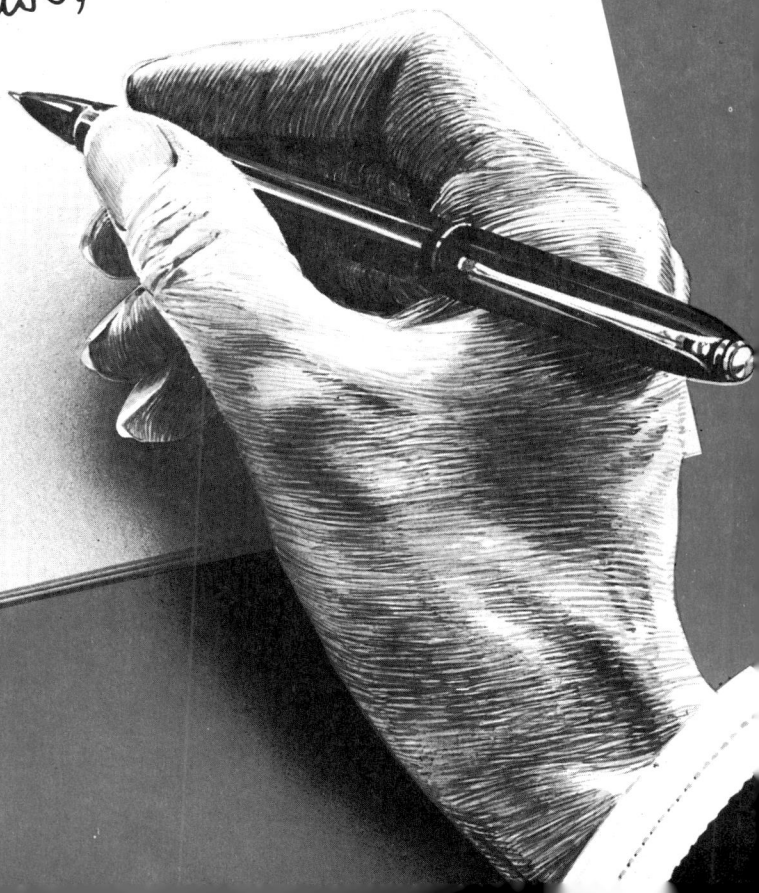

A personal chat with your tutor.

With Lesson 12, which demonstrates how to improve your spelling, we bring our course to a close. We hope that you have enjoyed studying it as much as we have enjoyed compiling and teaching it. Furthermore, we hope that you have found it beneficial and that, when you have worked through this final lesson, you will consider yourself well equipped to forge ahead on your own.

Finishing these lessons is naturally not the end of your use of English. The knowledge you have gained is going to stand you in good stead for the rest of your life. Its purpose is to qualify you to apply what you have learned to the various facets of your daily life where good English is necessary.

Based upon a long experience of teaching by correspondence, this course has been written to help you in your studies to the utmost of our ability. It attempts to point out how your goal can be achieved in the most economical and least laborious way.

I should like to assure you of my deep and sincere interest in your attaining the standard that you have set your sights on. I believe that your possession and use of these units will prove as rewarding an experience for you as preparing and editing them have proved for us.

If at any time you care to write and let me know about any success to which your new command of English has contributed, rest assured that your report will be read with the greatest of interest and pleasure. Can't you just imagine the warm glow of pride and satisfaction that will run through you when you sit down to pen such a letter? Of course you can!

Good luck to your future success!

Geoffrey A. Dudley

New Course in Practical English

Spelling Review for Adults

By Ann Arnold Sullivan, M.A.

Outline

© 1965 CAREER INSTITUTE, Inc. (English Edition)
© 1951
CAREER INSTITUTE, Inc.
First British Edition 1975
Printed in Great Britain
by
R. & W. Heap (Publishing) Co. Ltd., Marple, Cheshire

Spelling Review for Adults

THIS spelling review for adults is included in the Course in Practical English for two reasons. *First,* correct spelling is a requirement for accurate word–recognition and vocabulary–building. *Secondly,* spelling ability is vitally necessary if you are to write with confidence, ease, and speed.

To write a letter, report, or article that contains mis-spelt words is almost an unforgivable error. Frequent mis-spellings in business writing may prevent a person from being promoted to a position for which he is otherwise qualified. Mis-spellings in social correspondence often affect social standing because they create an impression of a lack of educational or cultural background.

Suggestions for Improvement

Learning to spell well is not difficult, particularly if you set up a spelling-improvement programme for yourself. The programme is simple and consists of the following steps:

1. **Learn the six basic spelling rules.** This unit presents these rules for you with practice exercises that will help you to learn and apply each rule. The rules for forming plurals, possessives, and contractions are also included.

2. **Keep a notebook of words you mis-spell.** Go over this list frequently until you are sure that you know the correct spelling of the words. You will be surprised how effective this notebook system will be and how little of your time it will take. After completing this spelling unit, continue keeping the notebook until you have learned to spell correctly the majority of words that you regularly use in your writing.

3. **Don't guess about the spelling of a word**—look it up in the dictionary. If you find that you have mis-spelt a word, add it to your spelling notebook. Looking up words in the dictionary takes a little time, but it prevents embarrassing mistakes.

4. **Try to picture any particularly difficult word in your mind's eye as well as to hear it with your mind's ear.** You can do this by writing the word to see how it looks in script as compared with the printed word. Then pronounce the word correctly to see if it is spelt as it sounds.

Definition of Terms

As you work through this unit, you will find that certain terms are used in giving rules or when referring to words. You will probably know the meanings of most of these words, but to make sure that they are clearly understood, they are defined below. Some of the terms, such as *root, prefix,* and *suffix,* have already been discussed in the Vocabulary Building units.

1. **Syllable**—A syllable is a word or a division of a word made by one or more speech sounds. Each syllable must contain one vowel sound. In addition to a vowel, the syllable may or may not contain one or more consonants.

Examples: *man* (one-syllable word) *jan.i.tor* (three syllables)

2. **Vowel**—The alphabet is composed of letters called *consonants* and *vowels.* The vowels are **a, e, i, o, u,** and sometimes **y.** The letter **y** is a vowel in the words *cycle, rhyme, lovely,* etc.

3. **Consonant**—The consonants include all the other letters in the alphabet besides the five vowels. The letter **y** is a consonant in the words *yet, yard, year,* etc.

4. **Root word**—The root or base of a word is the *main part* or body of the word. It is the part of the word that gives the essential or basic meaning. In the following examples, the root of each word is printed in bold type:

Root Word: *porto, portare*—to carry

trans**port**—carry across trans**port**ation—the act of carrying across

porter—one who carries ex**port**—carry out of the country

5. **Prefix**—A prefix is a word or group of letters attached to the *beginning* of a root word *to change* or *modify its meaning.* In the following examples the prefixes are in bold type:

Root Word: *video, videre*—to see or look

review—to see again **pro**vide—to look out for in advance

invisible—incapable of being seen **re**vision—the act of seeing again

6. **Suffix**—A suffix is a word or group of letters added to the *end* of a root word *to change* or *modify its meaning.* In the following examples, the suffixes are in bold type:

Root Word: *audio, audire*—to hear

audible—capable of being heard **aud**it—a formal examination

audience—act of listening **aud**itor—one who hears or listens

For further revision of root words, prefixes, and suffixes, refer to the Vocabulary Units of your course. It is suggested that you study carefully

Picture any particularly difficult word in your mind's eye as well as in your mind's ear.

the lists of prefixes and suffixes (and their meanings) you find there as an aid to spelling and word-recognition. Become "prefix and suffix conscious." Form the habit of seeing a word in its various parts instead of as a whole. The following exercise will test your ability to recognize word parts.

Exercise 1

Directions: In the words listed below, pick out the *root words* in the first column, the *prefixes* in the second column, and the *suffixes* in the third column. When you have finished, check your work with the answer key at the back of this book.

Root Word	Prefix	Suffix
Example: in**script**ion	**over**reach	dis**approval**
1. performance	1. submarine	1. remittance
2. assistance	2. supersede	2. supplication
3. convene	3. transoceanic	3. commentary
4. provoke	4. permission	4. milage
5. transferable	5. convince	5. socialist
6. perspective	6. promote	6. preferring
7. incredible	7. illegal	7. government
8. contractor	8. disturbance	8. progressive
9. preposition	9. circumscribe	9. courageous
10. durable	10. antecedent	10. likable

Basic Spelling Rules

In the following section, you will find the six basic spelling rules which will guide you in your programme of spelling improvement. Each rule is illustrated by an example, and exceptions (if any) are noted. Following each rule is an exercise which will enable you to test your understanding of the rule. Answers to the exercises are given in the key at the back of the booklet.

Rule 1. Words ending with a silent **e** usually drop the **e** before a suffix beginning with a vowel.

Root Word		Suffix		Complete Word
survive	+	al	=	survival
divide	+	ing	=	dividing
fortune	+	ate	=	fortunate
abuse	+	ive	=	abusive

Exceptions to the rule:

    a. Words containing the soft sounds of **g** or **c** retain the **e** before the suffixes **able** or **ous**. *Examples:* courageous, advantageous, peaceable, noticeable, changeable, manageable.

    b. Retain the **e** in words that might be mistaken for another word if the rule were applied. *Examples:* singe, singeing; dye, dyeing; shoe, shoeing; canoe, canoeing.

    c. Words ending in **ie** drop the **e** and change the **i** to **y** when the suffix **ing** is added. This is done to prevent two **i**'s from coming together. *Examples:* die, dying; tie, tying; lie, lying.

    d. In the word **mil(e)age**, the **e** may be retained before the suffix **age**. **Acreage** always retains it because in **acre** the **e** is not silent. In **lin(e)age**, the **e** is dropped or retained according to the meaning. **Linage** means number of lines; **lineage** means ancestry.

Exercise 2

Directions: Write the words formed by combining the words in the first column with the suffixes in the second column.

Word	Suffix
1. accumulate	ion
2. desire	ous
3. shoe	ing
4. mile	age
5. imitate	or
6. approve	al
7. change	able
8. dye	ing
9. peace	able
10. guide	ance
11. courage	ous
12. advise	ory
13. notice	able
14. acre	age
15. radiate	or
16. divide	ing
17. prepare	ation
18. outrage	ous
19. lie	ing
20. abuse	ive

Rule 2. Words ending with a silent **e** usually retain the **e** before a suffix beginning with a consonant.

Word		Suffix		Complete Word
arrange	+	ment	=	arrangement
forgive	+	ness	=	forgiveness
safe	+	ty	=	safety
shame	+	less	=	shameless

Exceptions to the rule: argue, argument; true, truly; nine, ninth; wise, wisdom; whole, wholly; awe, awful. Note, however, aweless and awesome, which comply with the rule. In the following words the e may be either dropped or retained: abridg(e)ment, acknowledg(e)ment, fledg(e)ling, judg(e)ment, and lodg(e)ment.

Exercise 3

Directions: Write the words formed by combining the words in the first column with the suffixes in the second column.

Word	Suffix
1. disgrace	ful
2. judge	ment
3. noise	less
4. acknowledge	ment
5. argue	ment
6. care	fully
7. wise	dom
8. true	ly
9. complete	ly

Lesson 12

Run + ing = running.

10. tire	less
11. force	ful
12. engage	ment
13. like	ness
14. positive	ly
15. announce	ment
16. awe	ful
17. arrange	ment
18. blame	less
19. immediate	ly
20. achieve	ment

Rule 3. Words of *one* syllable, ending in a *single* consonant preceded by a *single* vowel, double the final consonant before a suffix beginning with a vowel.

run	+	ing	=	running	clan	+	ish	=	clannish
big	+	est	=	biggest	plan	+	ing	=	planning
hot	+	er	=	hotter	bag	+	age	=	baggage

If the word ends with *two* or *more* consonants, or if the final consonant is preceded by *two* vowels instead of one, the rule does *not* apply.

		Two Consonants					**Two Vowels**		
debt	+	or	=	debtor	frail	+	est	=	frailest
yard	+	age	=	yardage	swear	+	ing	=	swearing
calm	+	est	=	calmest	sweet	+	er	=	sweeter

Exercise 4

Directions: Write the words formed by combining the words in the first column with the suffixes in the second column.

	Word	**Suffix**
1.	wrap	er
2.	thin	er
3.	tract	or
4.	spin	ing
5.	drug	ist
6.	clan	ish
7.	bag	age
8.	yard	age
9.	steep	est
10.	knit	ed
11.	treat	ing
12.	rid	ance
13.	tax	able
14.	freak	ish
15.	frail	est
16.	fiend	ish
17.	trim	ed
18.	moan	ing
19.	knock	ed
20.	hop	ing

Rule 4. Words of *two* or *more* syllables, accented on the final syllable and ending in a single consonant preceded by a single vowel, double the final consonant before a suffix beginning with a vowel. If the accent is *not* on the last syllable, the final consonant is *not* doubled.

Accent on Last Syllable				Accent Not on Last Syllable				
refer	+	ing	=	referring	benefit	+	ed	=	benefited
regret	+	able	=	regrettable	differ	+	ence	=	difference
occur	+	ence	=	occurrence	transfer	+	able	=	transferable

Exceptions to the rule:

a. If the final consonant is **l**, it is doubled regardless of the accent.

appal	+	ing	=	appalling
travel	+	er	=	traveller
But: parallel	+	ed	=	paralleled

b. If the final consonant is **s**, usage varies.

bias	+	ed	=	biased or biassed
focus	+	ed	=	focused or focussed
nonplus	+	ed	=	nonplussed
trellis	+	ed	=	trellised

If the word ends in *two* consonants, if the final consonant is preceded by *two* vowels, or if the accent shifts to the *first* syllable when the suffix is added, the rule does *not* apply.

perform	+	ance	=	performance	(two consonants)
repeal	+	ing	=	repealing	(two vowels)
refer	+	ence	=	reference	(accent shifts)

Exceptions to the rule.

Exercise 5

Directions: Write the words formed by combining the words in the first column with the suffixes in the second column.

Word	Suffix
1. commit	ed
2. appeal	ing
3. transfer	able
4. defer	ence
5. benefit	ed
6. begin	ing
7. forgot	en
8. defeat	ed
9. revolt	ing
10. perform	ance
11. occur	ence
12. resist	ance
13. conceal	ed
14. expel	ing
15. avoid	able
16. prefer	ence
17. annul	ed
18. travel	er
19. danger	ous
20. differ	ence

Rule 5. Use of "ei" and "ie." Use **i** before **e** except when the two letters follow **c** and have a long **e** sound, or when the two vowels are pronounced like long **a**.

Long e after c	Long a sound	After letters other than c
conceit	vein	shield
deceive	weight	believe

Lesson 12

ceiling   veil   grieve
receipt   freight   niece
perceive   neighbour   mischievous

Exceptions to the rule:

weird	foreign	seize	leisure
either	forfeit	height	ancient
neither	siege	surfeit	sovereign

Exercise 6

Directions: Complete the words in the list below by filling in **ie** or **ei**, whichever is correct.

1. conc__ted
2. bel__ve
3. handkerch__f
4. w__ght
5. n__ce
6. misch__f
7. rev__wing
8. s__ze
9. th__ves
10. w__ld
11. s__ge
12. sover__gn
13. cash__r
14. sh__ld
15. th__r
16. y__ld
17. n__ghbourhood
18. dec__ves
19. l__sure
20. fr__ght
21. r__n
22. sc__nce
23. rec__ver
24. sh__ld
25. h__rs
26. consc__nce
27. v__l
28. sl__gh
29. p__ce
30. perc__ve
31. rel__f
32. ach__vement
33. chandel__r
34. rec__pt
35. l__n
36. s__zure
37. shr__k
38. fr__nd
39. sl__ght-of-hand
40. f__nd
41. chiffon__r
42. br__f
43. r__gn
44. surf__t
45. c__ling
46. s__ve
47. f__gned
48. v__n
49. f__ld
50. counterf__t

Rule 6. Words ending in **y** preceded by a consonant usually change the **y** to **i** before any suffix *except* one beginning with an **i**.

beauty	+	ful	=	beautiful	accompany	+	ment	=	accompaniment
lady	+	es	=	ladies	accompany	+	ing	=	accompanying
lovely	+	ness	=	loveliness	ratify	+	es	=	ratifies

Exceptions to the rule:

shy	+	ness	=	shyness	lady	+	like	=	ladylike
baby	+	hood	=	babyhood	beauty	+	ous	=	beauteous
plenty	+	ous	=	plenteous	wry	+	ly	=	wryly

If the final **y** is preceded by a vowel, the rule does *not* apply.

journey	+	s	=	journeys	obey	+	ing	=	obeying
buy	+	s	=	buys	repay	+	ing	=	repaying
essay	+	s	=	essays	attorney	+	s	=	attorneys

Note: This rule will be referred to later in this unit in the section on forming plurals.

Exercise 7

Lesson 12
(Make notes in this margin
it helps you learn).

Directions: Write the words formed by combining the words in the first column with the suffixes in the second column.

Word	Suffix
1. annoy	ance
2. survey	or
3. verify	ing
4. lady	like
5. day	ly
6. heavy	est
7. delay	ing
8. quality	es
9. joy	ous
10. modify	es
11. donkey	s
12. ordinary	ly
13. beauty	ful
14. betray	al
15. forty	eth
16. boy	ish
17. industry	ous
18. apply	ing
19. convey	ance
20. copy	ing

Forming Plurals of Nouns

If a word is incorrectly pluralized, it is, of course, mis-spelt. There are fourteen rules for forming plurals listed here, together with examples and exceptions to the rules. Following the first six rules there will be an exercise to test you. Following the last eight rules will come another test. Later, in the mastery tests, you will have an opportunity to grade yourself on the application of all fourteen rules.

1. Plurals of most nouns are formed by adding s to the singular word.

Singular	Plural	Singular	Plural
bell	bells	pencil	pencils
college	colleges	tablet	tablets

2. When nouns end in y preceded by a consonant, the plural is formed by changing the y to i and adding es.

Final y preceded by a consonant:		Final y preceded by a vowel:	
Singular	**Plural**	**Singular**	**Plural**
baby	babies	valley	valleys
century	centuries	donkey	donkeys
lady	ladies	turkey	turkeys

Note: See Rule 6 under Basic Spelling Rules in this unit.

3. When nouns end in ch, sh, ss, s, x, or z, add es to form the plural.

Singular	Plural	Singular	Plural
dress	dresses	church	churches
fox	foxes	dish	dishes
gas	gases	quiz	quizes

Lesson 12

4. The plurals of nouns ending in **f**, **ff**, or **fe** are formed by adding **s** to the singular. However, some nouns with these endings change the **f** or **fe** to **v** and add **es.**

Add s for plural

Singular	Plural
cliff	cliffs
handkerchief	handkerchiefs
safe	safes

Change f to v and add es

Singular	Plural
wife	wives
leaf	leaves
self	selves

5. *(a)* The plurals of nouns ending in **o** preceded by a vowel are usually formed by adding **s** to the singular. Musical terms ending in **o** add **s** although the final **o** is not always preceded by a vowel.

Singular	Plural	Singular	Plural
studio	studios	piano	pianos
ratio	ratios	trio	trios
portfolio	portfolios	soprano	sopranos

(b) Nouns ending in **o** preceded by a consonant usually add **es** to form the plural.

Singular	Plural	Singular	Plural
motto	mottoes	hero	heroes
tomato	tomatoes	echo	echoes
potato	potatoes	Negro	Negroes

(c) Some nouns ending in **o** have two plural forms. In the following examples, the preferred plural form is given first:

Singular	Plural
memento	mementos or mementoes
banjo	banjoes or banjos
grotto	grottoes or grottos

6. *(a)* Plurals of compound nouns are formed by adding **s** to the most important word or most essential part of the compound.

Singular	Plural	Singular	Plural
sister-in-law	sisters-in-law	co-editor	co-editors
passer-by	passers-by	time-table	time-tables
editor-in-chief	editors-in-chief	washer-up	washers-up

(b) Sometimes both parts of a compound noun are made plural.

Example: manservant   menservants

Compounds ending in **ful** form the plural by adding **s** to the end of the compound.

Singular	Plural	Singular	Plural
cupful	cupfuls	handful	handfuls
spoonful	spoonfuls	tubful	tubfuls

(c) If there is no important word in the compound, or if both words are equal in importance, make the last part of the compound plural.

Singular	Plural
clothes-brush	clothes-brushes
charwoman	charwomen
wash-cloth	wash-cloths

Tomato + es = tomatoes.

Exercise 8

Directions: This exercise is based on the first six rules for forming plurals. Write the correct plural forms of the following words:

1. curio		16. piano	
2. tooth-brush		17. belief	
3. potato		18. rodeo	
4. dwarf		19. manservant	
5. mother-in-law		20. wish	
6. shelf		21. attorney	
7. holiday		22. box	
8. class		23. malady	
9. veto		24. hero	
10. elf		25. knife	
11. bench		26. enemy	
12. party		27. basement	
13. week-end		28. cello	
14. trade union		29. comedy	
15. chorus		30. patch	

7. Plurals of some nouns are formed by a change in the vowel or by a complete change of spelling.

Singular	Plural	Singular	Plural
man	men	foot	feet
child	children	woman	women
mouse	mice	goose	geese
ox	oxen	tooth	teeth

8. Some nouns have the same form in **both** the **singular** and **plural**.

Examples: athletics, corps, deer, fish, moose, sheep, species.

9. Some nouns are **always singular**. They have no plural form.

Examples: tennis, golf, music, offspring, status.

10. Some nouns are **always plural**. They have no singular form.

Examples: afters, offscourings, pliers, tongs, suds.

11. Some words derived from a foreign language retain their foreign plurals.

Singular	Plural	Singular	Plural
datum	data	analysis	analyses
alumnus	alumni (masculine)	synopsis	synopses
alumna	alumnae (feminine)	stratum	strata

Sometimes, however, the English plurals are used instead of the foreign plurals.

Singular	Plural
referendum	referendums
octopus	octopuses
villa	villas

12. The plurals of proper nouns are formed by adding **s** if the name does **not** end in **s**, or by adding **es** if the name ends in **s**.

1. There are two **Marys** in our family.
2. Three **Besses** answered the roll-call.
3. The **Adamses** have a new car.
4. The **Joneses** and the **Halls** are old friends.

13. Titles are made plural as follows: the plural of *Miss* is *Misses;* the plural of *Mr.* is *Messrs.* (abbreviation of *Messieurs*); and the word *Mrs.* has no plural. The plural of *Madam* is *Mesdames* and corresponds somewhat to a plural form for *Mrs.*

Note: Miss and *Misses* are not abbreviations and should not be followed by periods.

the Misses Allen or the Miss Allens

the Messrs. Johnson or the Mr. Johnsons

When listing a group of men, use *Messrs.* followed by the name of each man. When listing a group of married women, use *Mesdames* followed by the name of each woman. When listing unmarried women, use *Misses* followed by their names.

Messrs. or Messieurs Jones, Smith, Johnson, and Stevens.

Mesdames Allen, Lamson, Davis, and Wilson.

The Misses Dowd, Kelly, Arnold, and Sullivan.

14. Plurals of letters, symbols, and numbers are formed by adding an apostrophe and **s ('s)**.

Examples: A's   x's   2's   ?'s   +'s   £'s

Exercise 9

Directions: This exercise is based on the last eight rules for forming plurals. Write the correct plural forms of the following words:

1. crisis	14. Smith
2. stratum	15. ?
3. louse	16. Jones
4. axis	17. Miss
5. goose	18. freshman
6. shears	19. crocus
7. moose	20. datum
8. E	21. sheep
9. child	22. château
10. Sally	23. thesis
11. deer	24. chairman
12. Mr.	25. James
13. woman	26. parenthesis

Forming Possessives

The apostrophe (') is a mark used to show that a noun (or indefinite pronoun) is possessive, or to indicate a contraction. Just as a word is mis-spelt if it is pluralized incorrectly, so is it mis-spelt if the apostrophe is omitted or inserted in the wrong place in a word that shows possession.

1. If the *singular* form of the noun does not end in s, add the apostrophe and s ('s). If the singular ends in s, add the apostrophe (').

Note: In the possessive singular of nouns that end in s, if you want the *sound* of an additional s, the apostrophe and s ('s) may be added, especially if the noun has only one syllable.

Singular	Possessive	Singular	Possessive
boy	boy's	Harold	Harold's
child	child's	Davis	Davis' (or Davis'
Ross	Ross's	woman	woman's

2. If the *plural* does not end in s, add the apostrophe and s('s). If the plural ends in s, add the apostrophe (').

Helpful hint: Make the word plural first; then make it possessive.

Plural	Possessive	Plural	Possessive
calves	calves'	bosses	bosses'
boys	boys'	children	children's
men	men's	sheep	sheep's
weeks	weeks'	Joneses	Joneses'

The apostrophe is used to show that a noun (or indefinite pronoun) is possessive or to indicate a contraction.

Caution: Be sure that you always add the apostrophe to the end of a word and that you do not insert it within the word. For example, take the proper name Jones. If you insert the apostrophe before the s *(Jone's)*, it means that the proper name is *Jone.*

3. Possessive personal pronouns do *not* require an apostrophe.

my, mine	you, yours	he, his	they, theirs
it, its	we, ours	she, hers	who, whose

Note: It's is a contraction of *it is* or *it has* and not the possessive of *it.*

4. Possessives of indefinite pronouns are formed by adding an apostrophe and s ('s).

else's	someone's	everybody's
somebody's	everyone's	one's

5. Possession in a compound word is shown at the *end* of the word, regardless of which part of the compound may be pluralized.

Singular	**Singular Possessive**
tradesman	tradesman's
editor-in-chief	editor-in-chief's
secretary-treasurer	secretary-treasurer's

Plural	**Plural Possessive**
brothers-in-law	brothers-in-law's
menservants	menservants'
freshmen	freshmen's

Exercise 10

Directions: In the following sentences, supply the correct possessive form of the nouns enclosed in parentheses. Determine first whether the word should be singular or plural, according to the meaning of the sentence.

1. Mary and I sat at the (speaker) table.
2. The (city) playgrounds must be kept open.
3. We are celebrating (James) tenth birthday tomorrow.
4. Have you ever read (Dickens) "Christmas Carol"?
5. This year I shall have three (week) holiday.
6. The little (dog) tail wagged happily.
7. This is someone (else) coat, not mine.
8. Most (girl) manners are better than most (boy).
9. There is my (sister-in-law) house.
10. We have just completed three (day) work.
11. The (saleswoman) cash register was short.
12. (Calf) liver is on the menu every day.
13. The (foreman) plan was very successful.
14. I stayed all day with (Mrs. Adams) children.
15. All (chairman) reports will be given tonight.
16. The party honoured the (officer) wives.
17. The department store closed (it) doors at 5 p.m.
18. (Everyone) memory is not so good as hers.
19. The (child) appetites were enormous.
20. I am reading a book of (Burns) poems.

SUPPLY THE POSSESSIVE FORM

Forming Contractions

The second use of the apostrophe is to show the omission of one or more letters in words that are contracted.

it's (it is, it has)	doesn't (does not)	e'er (ever)
can't (cannot)	couldn't (could not)	isn't (is not)
don't (do not)	wouldn't (would not)	you're (you are)
I've (I have)	haven't (have not)	won't (will not)
I'm (I am)	hadn't (had not)	who's (who is, who has)

Caution: Possessives of personal pronouns have no apostrophe and should *not* be confused with contractions.

Examples: hers, its, his, theirs, yours, your, ours, etc.

Exercise 11

Directions: In the following sentences, supply the correct contraction of the words enclosed in parentheses. Remember that a word is mis-spelt if an apostrophe is omitted, or if one is inserted where it does not belong.

1. (I have) never been to York.
2. (Have not) I met you somewhere before?
3. The team tried but (could not) overcome the lead.
4. There is the man (who is) due to speak.
5. (Are not) you going to the dance tonight?
6. The child said he (would not) do it again.
7. The Johnson twins (do not) look much alike.
8. (You are) the first person to arrive.
9. We (cannot) remember the actor's name.
10. (I am) Mr. Martin's sister Jane.
11. The enemy (will not) surrender until they are crushed.
12. (It is) ten o'clock and past your bedtime.
13. The boy discovered that crime (does not) pay.
14. (Had not) you better call the police at once?
15. This (is not) the first time (you have) been late.
16. (They have) gone down to the beach every day this summer.
17. They think (we are) going to meet them.
18. I know that (he will) be late for the meeting.
19. (You will) be sorry if you miss the party.
20. It (is not) often that (they are) late.

Mis-Spellings Caused by Suffixes

Earlier in this unit, you learned certain basic spelling rules that applied to the addition of suffixes to words. However, since there are many widely used words where these rules do not apply, the following exercises will provide you with extra drill on the addition of suffixes. In the majority of cases, the spelling of the words is not governed by a rule.

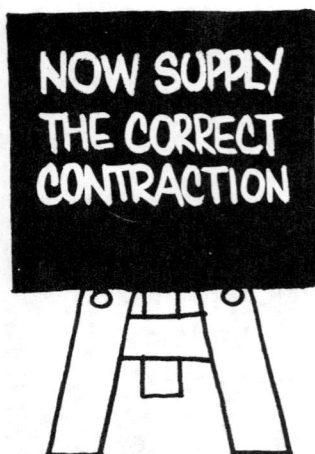

NOW SUPPLY THE CORRECT CONTRACTION

Exercise 12-Suffixes ant, ent

Directions: Add one of the endings **ant** or **ent**, whichever is correct, to complete the following words:

1. resist_____
2. relev_____
3. pleas_____
4. immin_____
5. import_____
6. suffici_____
7. vac_____
8. abs_____
9. perman_____
10. transi_____
11. transpar_____
12. assist_____
13. cli_____
14. incess_____
15. ten_____
16. compet_____
17. abund_____
18. adjac___-___
19. defi_____
20. reluct_____

21. emin_____
22. repent_____
23. superintend_____
24. observ_____
25. effici_____
26. occup_____
27. preval_____
28. descend_____
29. depend_____
30. ignor_____
31. account_____
32. gall_____
33. signific_____
34. warr_____
35. correspond_____
36. stimul_____
37. extravag_____
38. intellig_____
39. lieuten_____
40. conveni_____

Add the endings to these words.

Exercise 13-Suffixes ance, ence

Directions: Add one of the endings **ance** or **ence**, whichever is correct, to complete the following words. Don't forget to double the final consonant whenever necessary for correct spelling.

1. dist_____
2. inherit_____
3. resist_____
4. obedi_____
5. accept_____
6. pres_____
7. admit_____
8. independ_____
9. innoc_____
10. prefer_____
11. occur_____
12. entr_____
13. defi_____
14. toler_____
15. abund_____
16. audi_____
17. allow_____
18. hindr_____
19. leni_____
20. acquaint_____

21. interfer_____
22. perform_____
23. convey_____
24. reluct_____
25. hesit_____
26. temper_____
27. impati_____
28. observ_____
29. emin_____
30. perman_____
31. preval_____
32. import_____
33. neglig_____
34. remit_____
35. eloqu_____
36. sil_____
37. ignor_____
38. abs_____
39. confer_____
40. assist_____

Lesson 12

Exercise 14-Suffixes able, ible

Directions: Add one of the endings **able** or **ible**, whichever is correct, to complete the following words. Leave out all unnecessary letters, and double the consonant whenever necessary for correct spelling.

1. imposs _____	26. dishonour _____
2. accept _____	27. deplore _____
3. indel _____	28. perish _____
4. inelig _____	29. respect _____
5. incap _____	30. cure _____
6. vis _____	31. regret _____
7. impass _____	32. tax _____
8. invis _____	33. peace _____
9. admit _____	34. collapse _____
10. reli _____	35. predict _____
11. suit _____	36. adjust _____
12. irresist _____	37. endure _____
13. inevit _____	38. trace _____
14. syll _____	39. question _____
15. vulner _____	40. size _____
16. notice _____	41. sense _____
17. aud _____	42. digest _____
18. compar _____	43. adapt _____
19. prefer _____	44. credit _____
20. terr _____	45. redeem _____
21. flex _____	46. service _____
22. irrit _____	47. transfer _____
23. illeg _____	48. access _____
24. change _____	49. avail _____
25. like _____	50. laud _____

Exercise 15-Suffixes tion, sion, cian

Directions: Add one of the endings **tion**, **sion**, or **cian**, whichever is correct, to complete the following words:

1. satisfac _____	16. expedi _____
2. abbrevia _____	17. suspen _____
3. descrip _____	18. audi _____
4. occa _____	19. magi _____
5. musi _____	20. connec _____
6. excep _____	21. elimina _____
7. politi _____	22. deci _____
8. supervi _____	23. negotia _____
9. defini _____	24. consulta _____
10. transi _____	25. preten _____
11. expan _____	26. persua _____
12. admis _____	27. opti _____
13. separa _____	28. competi _____
14. inci _____	29. pronuncia _____
15. techni _____	30. revi _____

Learning can be fun!

Lesson 12
(Make notes in this margin
– it helps you learn).

Exercise 16-Suffixes ose, ous, ious, eous, uous

Directions: Add one of the endings, **ose, ous, ious, eous,** or **uous,** whichever is correct, to complete the following words:

1. rigor_____
2. humor_____
3. spac_____
4. plent_____
5. delic_____
6. gener_____
7. beaut_____
8. marvell_____
9. stud_____
10. tort_____
11. jeal_____
12. mischiev_____
13. miscellan_____
14. bellic_____
15. consc_____
16. numer_____
17. prev_____
18. joc_____
19. suspic_____
20. vigor_____
21. unanim_____
22. court_____
23. relig_____
24. grandi_____
25. ambit_____
26. mor_____
27. pretent_____
28. grac_____
29. prec_____
30. monoton_____

Exercise 17-Suffixes ise, ize, yse

Directions: Add one of the endings **ise, ize,** or **yse,** whichever is correct, to complete the following words:

1. advert_____
2. character_____
3. supr_____
4. patron_____
5. organ_____
6. recogn_____
7. comprom_____
8. penal_____
9. item_____
10. anal_____
11. exerc_____
12. legal_____
13. paral_____
14. surm_____
15. desp_____
16. modern_____
17. otherw_____
18. memor_____
19. superv_____
20. apolog_____
21. civil_____
22. steril_____
23. equal_____
24. adv_____
25. capital_____
26. idol_____
27. dramat_____
28. pasteur_____
29. emphas_____
30. merchand_____

Lesson 12
(Make notes in this margin
– it helps you learn).

Exercise 18-Suffixes
ar, er, or, our

Directions: Add one of the endings **ar**, **er**, **or**, or **our**, whichever is correct, to complete the following words:

1. auth_____	21. famili_____
2. act_____	22. operat_____
3. grant_____	23. examin_____
4. writ_____	24. superi_____
5. particul_____	25. may_____
6. janit_____	26. inspect_____
7. coll_____	27. advis_____
8. corn_____	28. visit_____
9. ang_____	29. elevat_____
10. trait_____	30. ancest_____
11. teach_____	31. success_____
12. past_____	32. travel_____
13. corrid_____	33. promot_____
14. charact_____	34. supervis_____
15. lavend_____	35. preach_____
16. calend_____	36. misdemean_____
17. bachel_____	37. administrat_____
18. gramm_____	38. cens_____
19. circul_____	39. cand_____
20. execut_____	40. mirr_____

Exercise 19-Suffixes al, el, le

Directions: Add one of the endings **al**, **el**, or **le**, whichever is correct, to complete the following words:

1. nick_____	21. lab_____
2. loc_____	22. fat_____
3. funn_____	23. bush_____
4. wrink_____	24. tick_____
5. fab_____	25. mort_____
6. journ_____	26. appar_____
7. manu_____	27. doub_____
8. coup_____	28. simp_____
9. identic_____	29. canc_____
10. person_____	30. trivi_____
11. chap_____	31. sing_____
12. peop_____	32. brut_____
13. vertic_____	33. nov_____
14. intern_____	34. vit_____
15. bicyc_____	35. trif_____
16. ax_____	36. coloss_____
17. tropic_____	37. personn_____
18. partic_____	38. profession_____
19. approv_____	39. cryst_____
20. assemb_____	40. entit_____

One Hundred Spelling Demons

Certain words are often mis-spelt because they are carelessly pronounced or have some peculiarity in spelling. Look at these words carefully, paying particular attention to the troublesome parts shown in **bold type**. This list contains words that are frequently mis-spelt.

1. government
2. across
3. chocolate
4. athletics (3 syllables)
5. su**r**prise
6. perspiration (not **pre**spiration)
7. library
8. environment
9. separate
10. accommodate
11. February
12. laboratory
13. wrestle
14. creek
15. catch
16. tragedy
17. Arctic
18. recognize (or recognise)
19. memory
20. representative
21. grammar
22. calendar
23. dictionary
24. captain
25. villain
26. poinsettia
27. pimento
28. paraffin
29. picnicking
30. supersede
31. preparation
32. embarrassed
33. occasion
34. Mediterranean
35. exhilarate
36. parliamentary
37. pamphlet
38. schedule
39. rhythm
40. business
41. ecstasy
42. exhibition
43. campaign
44. description
45. all right (2 words)
46. despair
47. privilege
48. sincerely
49. descendant
50. authorities
51. questionnaire
52. subtle
53. village
54. sandwich
55. superintendent
56. vicious
57. temporary
58. strategy
59. mischievous
60. manoeuvre
61. allege
62. accidentally
63. bulletin
64. auxiliary
65. judgment (or judgement)
66. guardian
67. truly
68. dissatisfied
69. nickel
70. liquefy
71. temperature
72. sacrilegious
73. conscience
74. conscious
75. prerogative
76. interrogate
77. occurrence
78. parallel
79. souvenir
80. apparel
81. etiquette
82. wizard
83. exhaust
84. Wednesday
85. colonel
86. sergeant
87. corporal
88. remembrance
89. temperament
90. literature
91. sacrifice
92. sentence
93. significant
94. affidavit
95. miniature
96. manufacture
97. candidate
98. salmon
99. definitely
100. equivalent

Look at these words carefully.

Lesson 12

Your scores will show
your degree of retention.

Mastery Test 1

These mastery tests should not be taken until a day or two after you have completed the exercises. The scores you make on the tests will then more clearly show your degree of retention.

Directions: Write the present participle (**ing** form) of the following verbs. Keep in mind the rules you have studied concerning doubling the final consonant and dropping the final silent **e**.

1. die (expire)	16. occur
2. lose	17. pretend
3. write	18. move
4. happen	19. dye (colour)
5. expel	20. choose
6. benefit	21. tie
7. owe	22. prefer
8. desire	23. spin
9. develop	24. interfere
10. admit	25. continue
11. cram	26. profit
12. promise	27. hope
13. defer	28. bleach
14. appeal	29. flirt
15. omit	30. repeat

Mastery Test 2

Directions: Write the words formed from the word elements and suffixes in the list below. Keep in mind the rules on the addition of suffixes that you studied earlier in this unit.

Word	Suffix
1. equip	ed
2. outrage	ous
3. consent	ed
4. conceal	ing
5. occur	ence
6. yard	age
7. shop	er
8. judge	ment
9. plan	ing
10. service	able
11. grieve	ous
12. likely	hood
13. country	s
14. admire	able
15. study	ing
16. approve	al
17. freak	ish
18. lonely	ness
19. prefer	ence
20. positive	ly
21. like	ness

22. remit   ance
23. credit   or
24. reveal   ing
25. peace   ful

Lesson 12
(Make notes in this margin
– it helps you learn).

Mastery Test 3

Directions: Write the correct plural forms of the following nouns:

1. tomato	16. tooth
2. cruelty	17. lens
3. fox	18. ceiling
4. brush	19. glass
5. studio	20. species
6. muff	21. ratio
7. foot	22. leaf
8. handful	23. sister-in-law
9. trio	24. cherub
10. journey	25. Wells
11. trench	26. alumnus
12. maidservant	27. Madam
13. basis	28. ottoman
14. handkerchief	29. Linda
15. salesman	30. Y

Mastery Test 4

Directions: Write the singular possessive, the plural, and the plural possessive of each of the following nouns and pronouns:

Singular
1. witness
2. it
3. chairman
4. month
5. child
6. editor-in-chief
7. Bess
8. sheep
9. vice-president
10. Negro
11. baby
12. Johnson
13. dwarf
14. co-editor
15. sheriff
16. I
17. hostess
18. alumna
19. secretary
20. wife

Mastery Test 5

Directions: In the first column, write the correct word combinations for the contractions. In the second column, write the correct contractions for the word combinations.

Contractions	Word Combinations
1. ne'er	11. would not
2. 'twas	12. it is
3. won't	13. they are
4. I've	14. are not
5. don't	15. should not
6. who'll	16. you have
7. e'er	17. did not
8. can't	18. of the clock
9. doesn't	19. who is
10. I'm	20. is not

Mastery Test 6

Directions: Write the correct spelling of any mis-spelt word in the list below. If no change is needed, write the word **correct**. There are **ten** words spelt correctly. These words are from the list of One Hundred Spelling Demons studied earlier in this unit.

1. chocalate	26. literature
2. accomodate	27. rememberance
3. accidently	· 28. exhilerate
4. judgment	29. temperment
5. wizzard	30. occurence
6. mischeivous	31. seperate
7. questionaire	32. laboratory
8. athletics	33. grammer
9. disatisfied	34. supercede
10. truely	35. corporal
11. nickle	36. parlamentary
12. liquify	37. ocassion
13. ettiquette	38. picnicing
14. affadavit	39. campaign
15. sergeant	40. poinsetta
16. villian	41. calender
17. alright	42. preparation
18. priviledge	43. embarassed
19. candidate	44. definitly
20. sincerly	45. minature
21. descendent	46. manufacture
22. representitive	47. villiage
23. aparrell	48. sacrafice
24. ecstacy	49. interogate
25. dictionery	50. Mediteranean

Correct? Well done!

Answer Key

Spelling Review

CORRECT ANSWERS TO EXERCISE 1

Root Words	Prefixes	Suffixes
1. performance	1. submarine	1. remittance
2. assistance	2. supersede	2. supplication
3. convene	3. transoceanic	3. commentary
4. provoke	4. permission	4. milage
5. transferable	5. convince	5. socialist
6. perspective	6. promote	6. preferring
7. incredible	7. illegal	7. government
8. contractor	8. disturbance	8. progressive
9. preposition	9. circumscribe	9. courageous
10. durable	10. antecedent	10. likable

CORRECT ANSWERS TO EXERCISE 2

1. accumulation	8. dyeing	15. radiator
2. desirous	9. peaceable	16. dividing
3. shoeing	10. guidance	17. preparation
4. mil(e)age	11. courageous	18. outrageous
5. imitator	12. advisory	19. lying
6. approval	13. noticeable	20. abusive
7. changeable	14. acreage	

CORRECT ANSWERS TO EXERCISE 3

1. disgraceful	8. truly	15. announcement
2. judg(e)ment	9. completely	16. awful
3. noiseless	10. tireless	17. arrangement
4. acknowledg(e)ment	11. forceful	18. blameless
5. argument	12. engagement	19. immediately
6. carefully	13. likeness	20. achievement
7. wisdom	14. positively	

CORRECT ANSWERS TO EXERCISE 4.

1. wrapper	8. yardage	15. frailest
2. thinner	9. steepest	16. fiendish
3. tractor	10. knitted	17. trimmed
4. spinning	11. treating	18. moaning
5. druggist	12. riddance	19. knocked
6. clannish	13. taxable	20. hopping
7. baggage	14. freakish	

Lesson 12
(Make notes in this margin
– it helps you learn).

Your Answer Key.

Lesson 12

CORRECT ANSWERS TO EXERCISE 5

1. committed
2. appealing
3. transferable
4. deference
5. benefited
6. beginning
7. forgotten
8. defeated
9. revolting
10. performance
11. occurrence
12. resistance
13. concealed
14. expelling
15. avoidable
16. preference
17. annulled
18. traveller
19. dangerous
20. difference

CORRECT ANSWERS TO EXERCISE 6

1. conceited
2. believe
3. handkerchief
4. weight
5. niece
6. mischief
7. reviewing
8. seize
9. thieves
10. wield
11. siege
12. sovereign
13. cashier
14. shield
15. their
16. yield
17. neighbourhood
18. deceives
19. leisure
20. freight
21. rein
22. science
23. receiver
24. shield
25. heirs
26. conscience
27. veil
28. sleigh
29. piece
30. perceive
31. relief
32. achievement
33. chandelier
34. receipt
35. lien
36. seizure
37. shriek
38. friend
39. sleight-of-hand
40. fiend
41. chiffonier
42. brief
43. reign
44. surfeit
45. ceiling
46. sieve
47. feigned
48. vein
49. field
50. counterfeit

CORRECT ANSWERS TO EXERCISE 7

1. annoyance
2. surveyor
3. verifying
4. ladylike
5. daily
6. heaviest
7. delaying
8. qualities
9. joyous
10. modifies
11. donkeys
12. ordinarily
13. beautiful
14. betrayal
15. fortieth
16. boyish
17. industrious
18. applying
19. conveyance
20. copying

CORRECT ANSWERS TO EXERCISE 8

1. curios
2. tooth-brushes
3. potatoes
4. dwarfs
5. mothers-in-law
6. shelves
7. holidays
8. classes
9. vetoes (or vetos)
10. elves
11. benches
12. parties
13. week-ends
14. trade unions
15. choruses
16. pianos
17. beliefs
18. rodeos
19. menservants
20. wishes
21. attorneys
22. boxes
23. maladies
24. heroes
25. knives
26. enemies
27. basements
28. cellos
29. comedies
30. patches

CORRECT ANSWERS TO EXERCISE 9

1. crises	14. Smiths
2. strata	15. ?'s
3. lice	16. Joneses
4. axes	17. Misses
5. geese	18. freshmen
6. shears	19. crocuses
7. moose *(singular and plural)*	20. data
8. E's	21. sheep *(singular and plural)*
9. children	22. châteaux
10. Sallys	23. theses
11. deer *(singular and plural)*	24. chairmen
12. Messrs. or Messieurs	25. Jameses
13. women	26. parentheses

CORRECT ANSWERS TO EXERCISE 10

1. Mary and I sat at the **speaker's** table.
2. The **city's** playgrounds must be kept open.
3. We are celebrating **James's** tenth birthday tomorrow.
4. Have you ever read **Dickens'** "Christmas Carol"? (or **Dickens's**)
5. This year I shall have three **weeks'** holiday.
6. The little **dog's** tail wagged happily.
7. This is someone **else's** coat, not mine.
8. Most **girls'** manners are better than most **boys'**.
9. There is my **sister-in-law's** house.
10. We have just completed three **days'** work.
11. The **saleswoman's** cash register was short.
12. **Calves'** liver is on the menu every Monday.
13. The **foreman's** plan was very successful.
14. I stayed all day with **Mrs. Adams'** children. (or **Adams's**)
15. All **chairmen's** reports will be given tonight.
16. The party honoured the **officers'** wives.
17. The department store closed **its** doors at 5 p.m.
18. **Everyone's** memory is not so good as **hers**.
19. The **children's** appetites were enormous.
20. I am reading a book of **Burns's** poems.

CORRECT ANSWERS TO EXERCISE 11

1. **I've** never been to York.
2. **Haven't** I met you somewhere before?
3. The team tried but **couldn't** overcome the lead.
4. There is the man **who's** due to speak.
5. **Aren't** you going to the dance tonight?
6. The child said he **wouldn't** do it again.
7. The Johnson twins **don't** look much alike.
8. **You're** the first person to arrive.
9. We **can't** remember the actor's name.
10. **I'm** Mr. Martin's sister Jane.
11. The enemy **won't** surrender until they are crushed.
12. **It's** ten o'clock and past your bedtime.
13. The boy discovered that crime **doesn't** pay.
14. **Hadn't** you better call the police at once?
15. This **isn't** the first time **you've** been late.
16. **They've** gone down to the beach every day this summer.

Lesson 12
(Make notes in this margin
– it helps you learn).

$$\frac{6}{10} \qquad \frac{9}{10}$$

$$\frac{8}{10} \qquad \frac{10}{10}$$

What's your score?

Lesson 12

(Make notes in this margin
— it helps you learn).

17. They think **we're** going to meet them.
18. I know that **he'll** be late for the meeting.
19. **You'll** be sorry if you miss the party.
20. It **isn't** often that **they're** late.

CORRECT ANSWERS TO EXERCISE 12

1. resistant
2. relevant
3. pleasant
4. imminent
5. important
6. sufficient
7. vacant
8. absent
9. permanent
10. transient
11. transparent
12. assistant
13. client
14. incessant
15. tenant
16. competent
17. abundant
18. adjacent
19. defiant
20. reluctant
21. eminent
22. repentant
23. superintendent
24. observant
25. efficient
26. occupant
27. prevalent
28. descendant
29. dependent (or dependant)
30. ignorant
31. accountant
32. gallant
33. significant
34. warrant
35. correspondent
36. stimulant
37. extravagant
38. intelligent
39. lieutenant
40. convenient

CORRECT ANSWERS TO EXERCISE 13

1. distance
2. inheritance
3. resistance
4. obedience
5. acceptance
6. presence
7. admittance
8. independence
9. innocence
10. preference
11. occurrence
12. entrance
13. defiance
14. tolerance
15. abundance
16. audience
17. allowance
18. hindrance
19. lenience
20. acquaintance
21. interference
22. performance
23. conveyance
24. reluctance
25. hesitance
26. temperance
27. impatience
28. observance
29. eminence
30. permanence
31. prevalence
32. importance
33. negligence
34. remittance
35. eloquence
36. silence
37. ignorance
38. absence
39. conference
40. assistance

CORRECT ANSWERS TO EXERCISE 14

1. impossible
2. acceptable
3. indelible
4. ineligible
5. incapable
6. visible
7. impassable (or impassible)
8. invisible
9. admirable
10. reliable
11. suitable
12. irresistible
13. inevitable
14. syllable
15. vulnerable
16. noticeable
17. audible
18. comparable
19. preferable
20. terrible
21. flexible
22. irritable
23. illegible
24. changeable
25. likable
26. dishonourable
27. deplorable
28. perishable
29. respectable
30. curable
31. regrettable
32. taxable
33. peaceable
34. collapsible (or collapsable)
35. predictable
36. adjustable
37. endurable
38. traceable
39. questionable
40. sizable
41. sensible
42. digestible
43. adaptable
44. creditable
45. redeemable
46. serviceable
47. transferable
48. accessible
49. available
50. laudable

Lesson 12

Aim for high scores.

CORRECT ANSWERS TO EXERCISE 15

1. satisfaction
2. abbreviation
3. description
4. occasion
5. musician
6. exception
7. politician
8. supervision
9. definition
10. transition
11. expansion
12. admission
13. separation
14. incision
15. technician
16. expedition
17. suspension
18. audition
19. magician
20. connection
21. elimination
22. decision
23. negotiation
24. consultation
25. pretension
26. persuasion
27. optician
28. competition
29. pronunciation
30. revision

CORRECT ANSWERS TO EXERCISE 16

1. rigorous
2. humorous
3. spacious
4. plenteous
5. delicious
6. generous
7. beauteous
8. marvellous
9. studious
10. tortuous (or tortious)
11. jealous
12. mischievous
13. miscellaneous
14. bellicose
15. conscious
16. numerous
17. previous
18. jocose
19. suspicious
20. vigorous
21. unanimous
22. courteous
23. religious
24. grandiose
25. ambitious
26. morose
27. pretentious
28. gracious
29. precious
30. monotonous

CORRECT ANSWERS TO EXERCISE 17

(Note: Nos. 2, 4-6, 8, 9, 12, 16, 18, 20-23, and 25-29 can also be spelt with *ise*.)

1. advertise
2. characterize
3. surprise
4. patronize
5. organize
6. recognize
7. compromise
8. penalize
9. itemize
10. analyse
11. exercise
12. legalize
13. paralyse
14. surmise
15. despise
16. modernize
17. otherwise
18. memorize
19. supervise
20. apologize
21. civilize
22. sterilize
23. equalize
24. advise
25. capitalize
26. idolize
27. dramatize
28. pasteurize
29. emphasize
30. merchandise

CORRECT ANSWERS TO EXERCISE 18

1. author
2. actor
3. grantor
4. writer
5. particular
6. janitor
7. collar
8. corner
9. anger
10. traitor
11. teacher
12. pastor
13. corridor
14. character
15. lavender
16. calendar
17. bachelor
18. grammar
19. circular
20. executor
21. familiar
22. operator
23. examiner
24. superior
25. mayor
26. inspector
27. adviser
28. visitor
29. elevator
30. ancestor
31. successor
32. traveller
33. promoter
34. supervisor
35. preacher
36. misdemeanour
37. administrator
38. censor (or censer)
39. candour
40. mirror

Lesson 12

(Make notes in this margin – it helps you learn).

CORRECT ANSWERS TO EXERCISE 19

1. nickel
2. local
3. funnel
4. wrinkle
5. fable
6. journal
7. manual
8. couple
9. identical
10. personal
11. chapel
12. people
13. vertical
14. internal
15. bicycle
16. axle
17. tropical
18. particle
19. approval
20. assemble
21. label
22. fatal
23. bushel
24. tickle
25. mortal
26. apparel
27. double
28. simple
29. cancel
30. trivial
31. single
32. brutal
33. novel
34. vital
35. trifle
36. colossal
37. personnel
38. professional
39. crystal
40. entitle

CORRECT ANSWERS TO MASTERY TEST 1

1. dying
2. losing
3. writing
4. happening
5. expelling
6. benefiting
7. owing
8. desiring
9. developing
10. admitting
11. cramming
12. promising
13. deferring
14. appealing
15. omitting
16. occurring
17. pretending
18. moving
19. dyeing
20. choosing
21. tying
22. preferring
23. spinning
24. interfering
25. continuing
26. profiting
27. hoping
28. bleaching
29. flirting
30. repeating

CORRECT ANSWERS TO MASTERY TEST 2

1. equipped
2. outrageous
3. consented
4. concealing
5. occurrence
6. yardage
7. shopper
8. judg(e)ment
9. planning
10. serviceable
11. grievous
12. likelihood
13. countries
14. admirable
15. studying
16. approval
17. freakish
18. loneliness
19. preference
20. positively
21. likeness
22. remittance
23. creditor
24. revealing
25. peaceful

CORRECT ANSWERS TO MASTERY TEST 3

1. tomatoes
2. cruelties
3. foxes
4. brushes
5. studios
6. muffs
7. feet
8. handfuls
9. trios
10. journeys
11. trenches
12. maidservants
13. bases
14. handkerchiefs
15. salesmen
16. teeth
17. lenses
18. ceilings
19. glasses
20. species *(singular and plural)*
21. ratios
22. leaves
23. sisters-in-law
24. cherubs (or cherubim)
25. Wellses
26. alumni
27. Mesdames
28. ottomans
29. Lindas
30. Y's

CORRECT ANSWERS TO MASTERY TEST 4

Singular Possessive	Plural	Plural Possessive
1. witness' (s)	witnesses	witnesses'
2. its	they	their, theirs
3. chairman's	chairmen	chairmen's
4. month's	months	months'
5. child's	children	children's
6. editor-in-chief's	editors-in-chief	editors-in-chief's
7. Bess's	Besses	Besses'
8. sheep's	sheep	sheep's
9. vice-president's	vice-presidents	vice-presidents'
10. Negro's	Negroes	Negroes'
11. baby's	babies	babies'
12. Johnson's	Johnsons	Johnsons'
13. dwarf's	dwarfs	dwarfs'
14. co-editor's	co-editors	co-editors'
15. sheriff's	sheriffs	sheriffs'
16. my, mine	we	our, ours
17. hostess' (s)	hostesses	hostesses'
18. alumna's	alumnae	alumnae's
19. secretary's	secretaries	secretaries'
20. wife's	wives	wives'

CORRECT ANSWERS TO MASTERY TEST 5

1. never
2. it was
3. will not
4. I have
5. do not
6. who will
7. ever
8. cannot
9. does not
10. I am
11. wouldn't
12. it's
13. they're
14. aren't
15. shouldn't
16. you've
17. didn't
18. o'clock
19. who's
20. isn't

CORRECT ANSWERS TO MASTERY TEST 6

1. chocolate
2. accommodate
3. accidentally
4. *correct*
5. wizard
6. mischievous
7. questionnaire
8. *correct*
9. dissatisfied
10. truly
11. nickel
12. liquefy
13. etiquette
14. affidavit
15. *correct*
16. villain
17. all right
18. privilege
19. *correct*
20. sincerely
21. descendant
22. representative
23. apparel
24. ecstasy
25. dictionary
26. *correct*
27. remembrance
28. exhilarate
29. temperament
30. occurrence
31. separate
32. *correct*
33. grammar
34. supersede
35. *correct*
36. parliamentary
37. occasion
38. picnicking
39. *correct*
40. poinsettia
41. calendar
42. *correct*
43. embarrassed
44. definitely
45. miniature
46. *correct*
47. village
48. sacrifice
49. interrogate
50. Mediterranean

CONGRATULATIONS

Congratulations! You've finished the Course. Your use of English will have improved dramatically. Now put what you've learned into practice!

New Course in Practical English

Lesson 12

Finally, here is a simple and enjoyable programme for improving your spelling.... to help you to write with confidence, ease, and speed!